Hope this ... —
cabin of your dreams!

Happy Birthday
😊

Love, Kathy & Stan

the cabin book

the cabin book

Linda Leigh Paul

UNIVERSE

First published in the United States of America in 2004
by UNIVERSE PUBLISHING
A Division of Rizzoli International Publications, Inc.
300 Park Avenue South
New York, NY 10010
www.rizzoliusa.com

2008 2009/ 10 9 8 7 6 5 4

Designed by Lynne Yeamans/Lync

Printed in China

ISBN : 978-0-7893-1192-4

Library of Congress Catalog Control Number: 2004110346

Acknowledgments

A trip to the cabin can mean anything thing from a private meditation to a weekend of skiing and sköl! On the slopes, at the lake, or in the woods, the cabin is a last resort; a vacation from vacations. It is the place where simple acts—chopping water, carrying wood, playing music, hunting mushrooms, making a meal—are done for their own sakes. There thoughts unfold as whole and blissful in themselves. The cabin: we are caught up with the immediate, the direct robustness of life and nature. How the heart can rise to pure poetry from what is thought of as the humblest of shelters.

My appreciation to the cabin owners for their participation in this book is immeasurable. Many shared their treasured, private places; others shared the chain of ownership of their cabin. All have shared a reverence for the landscape in which they live their cabin lives. For architects who inspire and share their client's visions, the completed projects are themselves, their own best reward. I owe a debt of gratitude to Anthony Belluschi, F.A.I.A., for providing a wealth of detailed information about his Dunes cabin; Paul Schlachter of Bohlin Cywinski Jackson for his insight on several projects; Dawn Fritz and Historical Concepts for contributing the Tew Barn project; Ligeia Uker for her contributions from Meyer, Scherer & Rockcastle, Ltd. The intuition and grace of the architectural photographers fill these pages, particularly to François Robert, for his manifest grace. This book is possible because of such dedication, for which I am deeply and admiringly grateful.

I wish to thank editor Holly Rothman for taking the lead on this project and bringing it to completion with visionary humor and style. Her eye for detail, her measured patience, and meticulous perspectives are heartily appreciated and gratefully received. I also want to thank Lynne Yeamans/Lync. for designing this book and for her intuitiveness and talent. And everyone else Holly brought together to work on this book. To Charles Miers, Rizzoli/Universe's extraordinary publisher, thank you once again for giving me the opportunity to work with Universe.

And to Robert Paul, I can't go anywhere without you.

CONTENTS

INTRODUCTION

" . . . we enjoyed many an adventure hunting ducks from an air boat in the Glades; diving the reefs off Lauderdale to stock the fish tank for flying to Bimini and a wild weekend snorkeling for lobster. The gang had three boats and three aircraft. My friend had acreage in the Carolinas, too. He and I would fly up on weekends and work on his old cabin . . ."

Letter from my father, 1999

Originally a cabin meant a new beginning. Now it is a literal last resort. We dream of an idyllic spot on earth where a warm, cozy cabin waits—where, perhaps, an elk herd might wander past, or falling snow will build heavy, biomorphic sculptures outside the window, and luminous streamers of the aurora borealis will hold us spellbound in the night. The attractions of "going to the cabin" are found in its surroundings: Inspiration and imagination are ignited by mountains, flatlands, meadows, valleys, high deserts, rivers, lakes, and of course, the ever-changing sky.

Such visits " . . . stimulate the aesthetic palate . . ."[1] The allure of stories told by those who have spent time on remote islands, climbed brutal mountains, were lost in the bush, or have walked through the desert, have an aesthetic, even ethical appeal. In these places we allow things to get close to us, and they *can* get close: Adam Nicolson writes with awe of the sound of the hundreds of thousands of puffins, kittiwakes, shags, and skuas nesting on a remote island.[2] In his book, *The Journey Home*, Edward Abbey writes longingly of the disappearing habitat of the moose and calf, badger, grizzly, and loon. He recalls a golden eagle that soared *below* their two-room cabin at timberline, seven thousand feet above sea level in Glacier

(Opposite) Bright light illuminates a small cabin in Jasper National Park's Tonquin Valley. Star trails streak the sky above. Photographer: Raymond Gehman

(*Left*) Aurora Borealis (*Opposite*) *On Time, Off Time*, by Dorothea Tanning, 1910-present. Photographer: Sanford/Angliolo

National Park. Dorothea Tanning writes in her recent autobiography, *Between Lives*, of her time in Sedona, Arizona, and the impossibility of painting large canvases in the "hum of the heat . . . so intense, so lurking . . ." that they lived as if they were "in peril." Yet she was able to paint "On Time, Off Time" in 1948, an image that brings to mind the heavenly cabin that she and Max Ernst built, and the hells it survived.

* * *

When Frank Lloyd Wright explored the possibilities of cabin design, it was 1923 and his palette was a pristine Lake Tahoe. The setting included Emerald Bay, forested slopes, an island in the lake, meadows—every imaginable cabin setting. His aim was to "bring the lake more fully within the scheme" of the design. His plan was a site that featured different types of cabins, including the floating cabin, which, true to its name, floated on the lake. He also planned the first

hexagonal cabin, with a steeply pitched roof and a compact but dynamic variation of lodge architecture for a flat site. Sadly, the project never went beyond a few drawings of cabins that he named: the "Barge for Two"; "Fallen Leaf"; and the powerful "Shore Cabin." Five years later, Wright was working out some wonderful angularities for cabins in the Arizona desert. He was taken by the desert landscape and wrote to his son, John, "There could be nothing more

(*Opposite*) This Fallen Leaf drawing is an original 1920s Frank Lloyd Wright illustration, shown prior to the conservation measures of the late 1980s. Fallen Leaf was a one-room floating cabin with an origami-patterned and peaked roof. (*Right*) 1920s cabins were all given names evocative of their appearance or location. The Shore Cabin would have been built on a flat site on the shore adjacent to the bay, and does feature large "bay" rooms.

inspiring on earth than that spot in the pure desert of Arizona . . ."[3] where he created a few cabins for his assistants at *Ocatilla*, their first camp in Arizona.

Wright, like us all, owes an allegiance to the early American cabins and the idealism that accompanies them: Abraham Lincoln reading next to a candle, Emerson's *Self-Reliance*, Thoreau's learning to live "deliberately." The purpose of architecture, though, is to incorporate into the design and the function of a building the reason for it being where one has chosen it to be. Concerns about cabins must include why or how a certain place was selected. A cabin is never solely about the architecture; it is always about where the architecture is placed and how well the cabin expresses that placement. Wright believed in and sought meaning from design's adherence to place—so much so that he distinguished "his geometries not only to achieve an individual bond with each specific location . . . but to complete that location's underlying structure, so that each place [becomes] more fully revealed as an indivisible part of the ordered cosmos."[4] Wright's twenties work with the cabins marks a subtle change in his design theory. The modernist world is present, along with the use of its materials and the ease of movement into and throughout the landscape.

* * *

Cabin design should free us. If the setting is harsh in the extreme, or a perfect paradise, a freedom from our usual obligations changes the way we think and feel. When, in 1913, the philosopher Ludwig Wittgenstein was exhausted by work and distracted by life at Cambridge, he found solitude in a rustic cabin in Skoldjen, a small village in Norway, "where he could be himself without the strain of upsetting or offending people. He could devote himself entirely to himself—or rather, to what he felt to be practically the same thing, to his logic . . . the beauty of the countryside . . . long solitary walks, relaxation, and meditation which produced in him a kind of euphoria. Together they created the perfect conditions in which to think. Looking back years later he would say, "*Then* my mind was on fire!"[5]

Every place, every setting, has its own particular genius, something about it that allows people to make it their own, something that allows people to learn to be happy there. This is the main ingredient in the recipe of the design process. The spirit of the site rises through the foundations of the design, through the earth, and spreads into the air. A cabin should say privacy, or solitude or excitement. It must be a response to the nature that embraces it.

The poet Gary Snyder lives in the forests of the Sierra Nevada. He has lived with his family amid the moods and cycles of weather, in harmony with the animals and birds, for more than thirty years. Snyder is a steward of the environment, living so deep within unspoiled nature that he has come to know how it can help one find the "wild mind," which for him is the heart of self-reliance. It has been challenging: "We figured that simplicity would of itself be beautiful, and we had our own extravagant notions of ecological morality. But necessity was the teacher that finally showed us how to live as part of the natural community. . . . We may not transform reality, but we may transform ourselves. And if we transform ourselves, we might just change the world a bit."[6]

(*Opposite*) Drawing of the Barge For Two. Intended to float or be anchored on the lake, the barge featured a kitchen and an open main level with a sheltered outdoor sleeping deck.

(*Left*) Blue and green color added during photographic processing add a bio-geometric glow to these stone cabins, lit from within by yellow light. Valley of Fire State Park, Nevada. Photographer: Richard Cummins

* * *

The cabins presented in this book represent their owners' willingness to explore and celebrate the verities of landscape, the "wild mind," recreation, and architecture, and the ways in which these speak to one another. Old log cabins have been cared for and have grown small but respectful additions. New log and other vernacular cabins have been designed to recall an era or style. One lovely retreat was designed and built in honor of an old barn, for an owner who cherished childhood memories. Several examples of architectural innovation and power still allow the architecture to be subordinate to the landscape. Some sanctuaries have elaborately finished interiors but regardless of their luxury they too respect their sites. Some are

dynamic displays of engineering and boldly reflect the need to withstand the surrounding terrain or local climate. There are cabins outfitted with all the comforts of home, yet their owners look forward to leaving home to be in them. It is from the cabin, whatever its design or furnishings, that the voices and shapes of Nature are known. Each cabin speaks of a personal style: rugged, gentle, creative, refined, intellectual, athletic. So splash your toes in the lake; put on your skis; catch that salmon; play your flute on the porch; or simply listen to the birds for hours. The cabin is the past, present, and future.

(*Above*) The exterior of writer and conservationist Sigurd Olson's cabin at Listening Point, Ely, Minnesota. Mr. Olson named one of his books after the Burntside Lake cabin. Photographer: Layne Kennedy (*Opposite*) Diverse and sparse furniture decorates an austere split log cabin in Marietta, Ohio. Photographer: Karen Tweedy-Holmes

ENDNOTES
1   Yi-Fu Tuan, *Topophilia: A Study of Environmental Perception, Attitudes, and Values* (Columbia University Press: New York, 1990), p. 114.
2   *Frank Lloyd Wright Quarterly*, Volume 7, Number 3, Summer 1996 (The Frank Lloyd Wright Foundation: Scottsdale), p. 15.
3   Ibid.
4   Ray Monk and Ludwig Wittgenstein, *The Duty of Genius* (The Free Press: New York, 1990), p.94.
5   John Miller and Aaron Kenedi, *Where Inspiration Lives: Writers, Artists, and Their Creative Places* (New World Library: Novato, 2003), p. 54.

PART I   Perfect Dependence

(*Opposite*) The cabin and screened porch are comforted in the greenery of the mountain and meadow. (*Right*) Rusted metal on the steeply sloping roof and porch, on the dormers and above the chimney, enhances the peacefulness of the cabin and the site.

COLORADO LOG CABIN

OWNERS: Robert and Beverly Trusheit
ARCHITECT: Charles Cunniffe Architects
PHOTOGRAPHER: Tim Murphy

This prototypical Colorado cabin is tucked into the tree line near Steamboat Springs. Overlooking the open meadows of wildflowers and hilly distances, the views take in the blue and changing surface of the large and cold mountain lake—Lake Catamount. Designed and sited to appear as the original log homestead, the architect detailed large-timber framing, exposed rafters, and log slab siding with chinking visible inside and out. Also essential was the stone base and the rusted-metal roofing material. The owners live comfortably in their cozy home, while their plans for a mountain ranch, including a barn, take shape.

The cabin interior is warm and offers an intimate greeting in the open living space. The room is focused around the prominent stone floor-to-ceiling fireplace. The elevation of the great-room ceilings confers a generous spaciousness to the modest floor plan. Thoughtful placement of windows allows natural light and "snow shine" to fill the room from every direction. The play of light alters the interior experiences and sensations throughout the day and the changing seasons in the high mountains. Well-appointed fabrics, rugs, and finish trim harken to a western past, while maintaining the warmth of a family home.

The cabin also features several spaces for the enjoyment of the outdoors. The front porch is a good place to relax and take in the morning and evening light. A lovely screened porch of timbers and stone is an extension of the great room. From this outdoor room the views and fragrances of the meadow, lake, and forest are within reach. A patio at the back of the cabin runs adjacent to the breezeway that connects the cabin to the garage. It is enclosed with a natural boulder wall and trees, and invites the entire interior living space of the cabin to enjoy an outdoor experience.

(Upper left) Views from the smooth stone cabin porch, over the meadow and hills, show Lake Catamount in the distance. (Lower right) The area on the stair landing is used for a game of chess or checkers or as a private place to read. (Lower left) Large open kitchen and bar is counterpoint to the smaller, more intimate dining area which features bay window seating. (Opposite) Living spaces are defined by height, light, and perspective. Select amenities make a cozy room feel spacious.

(Opposite) Built on the stony outcropping of glacial rock, the cabin faces the waters of the Strait of Georgia. *(Right)* The cabin "floats" on piers above the rock, where evergreens sprout around the wraparound porch.

CORTES ISLAND CABIN

OWNERS: Anonymous
ARCHITECT: Greg Robinson, AIA, The Cascade Joinery
PHOTOGRAPHER: J. K. Lawrence

Cortes Island is one of the many islands located between the mainland of British Columbia and Vancouver Island. The only way to reach it is by ferry or private boat from the Campbell River. No commercial center exists there, and there are very few roads. On a rocky point facing southwest, protruding into the aquamarine-green waters of the Strait of Georgia, is a getaway cabin inserted into the landscape.

For years the owners have spent their summers here in a cramped rustic cabin built in the early seventies by a previous owner. As the new owners' family grew, and more guests arrived, they desired a smaller cabin where they could get away to relax from all the activities and pursue their individual interests in music and painting. The solution is the lovely 660-square-foot building on top of the rocky point. Built for summer use only, the generous use of French doors, which open onto a ten-foot-wide wraparound porch, extends the usable space to the outdoors. The cabin is surrounded with functional spaciousness it otherwise would not have. The French doors, large transoms, and gable-end windows fill the interior with natural light while the wraparound porch eliminates a glare that is quite disruptive to painting.

The location of the cabin had, of course, a significant influence upon the design. The rocky knoll and the absence of vehicle access made excavation impractical. The solution was to support the entire structure on concrete piers that were anchored to the rock. The overall effect is one of the cabin floating above the glacial rock and velvet moss below. All timbers were fabricated off site and delivered by helicopter from Campbell River. The entire frame was completely erected within four days. As a result, the site showed no evidence of disturbance. The simple and beautiful cabin lives in this remote and spectacular natural setting with no alteration to the natural landscape.

(Left) French doors open to the ten-foot-wide porch where the cabin reaches into the landscape. *(Upper right)* The large, light, and airy living room is encompassed in vignettes of island life in the Northwest. *(Lower right)* Simplify and the universe will grant time to think.

Strong, simple, and deliberate, the
timber-frame cabin is a summer refuge.

(*Opposite*) The old cabin and gazebo addition in the treetops. (*Right*) A glance inside.

DUNE ACRES CABIN

OWNERS: Anthony and Marti Belluschi
ARCHITECTS: Alden Studebaker,
Anthony Belluschi, FAIA
PHOTOGRAPHER: Bob Shimer,
Hedrich Blessing Photography

Lake Michigan turns north in the upper-northwest corner of Indiana, where a significant lakescape of dunes exists. Dunes, formed at the edge of the water by wind and sand, are found as much as a mile inland up and down on the Michigan shore of this Great Lake. Dr. Henry Chandler Cowles, a nineteenth-century biologist, believed that the dunes in this area were formed in response to the winds carrying sand, which collided first with small obstacles, then gradually larger forms of plant life. First, the sands lodged in and among the crevasses of sea grasses; then, into the roots of small trees; and, finally, in and around

larger deciduous and evergreen trees, as the dunes continued to build. The ecologically sensitive area was recognized by Cowles as "a dynamic ecosystem, with land forms and micro-climates supporting more plant diversity per acre than in any other national park in the United States."[1]

Anthony Belluschi discovered his northwest-Indiana cabin just forty-six miles from his Chicago townhouse. Surrounded by the "living laboratory" of the Indiana Dunes State Park, the immediate area, too, has a history. The dune lands included "Cowles Bog," which was at the center of what one editor of the *Chesterton Tribune,* on

June 5, 1890, described as, "without one bit of exaggeration, the most godforsaken place in the State of Indiana . . . in the midst of sand hills, swamps and sloughs and headquarters for malaria, sand burs, and bullfrogs."

Nonetheless, the dunes became a community called Dune Acres. Almost all of the log houses in Dune Acres, prior to 1941, were built by a young man who arrived by motor-cycle in 1924 on Armistice Day, Alden Studebaker; he designed many more. The strong cedar logs came from Oregon and had to be precise in shape and taper to fit together properly.

The moment Anthony walked into the Circle Drive cabin, it made its claim on him. Built in 1932, the cathedral ceiling and large stone fireplace, combined with the Oregon logs, reminded him of a ski lodge at Mt. Hood, in Oregon, his home state. The logs were first placed on the floor and shaped manually with an adz to provide a flat mating surface between logs. The logs were then hoisted into place and spiked together. The joint was packed with oakum, a creosote-soaked, loosely woven hemp rope, using a wooden caulking tool, and malled.

Shortly after purchasing the cabin in 1991, Anthony married Marti, and today they spend as many days away in their private haven as their demanding schedules allow. He completed a small cedar-and-glass addition. The Belluschis are calmed by the views of the lake to the north, which often recall times lived, prior to moving to Chicago, on the East and West coasts. The lake can stir up waves and swells as high and fierce as any ocean. For the Belluschis, "there is nothing more basic" than watching the water from a log house amid the evergreens of the high dunes.

(Upper left) Addition of deck, bridge, and gazebo to the original cabin plan projects summer leisure and dining into the trees and over the valley. *(Upper right)* Alden Studebaker designed and built the cabin, shown here around 1932 when it's about to receive its roof. *(Opposite)* Studebaker's original beam and timber framing, with the original log walls, fill the interiors with an ageless charm.

(*Above*) The bridge to the gazebo, which
has a contemporary rusticity, surpasses
the cabin's attachment to history.
(*Right*) Anthony and Marti's terracing,
landscaping, and architectural transforma-
tions preserve Alden Studebaker's vision
in this idyllic spot.

ENDNOTES

1   Jerry Dennis, *The Living Great Lakes: Searching for the Heart of the Inland Seas*
    (St. Martin's Press: New York, 2003), pp. 58–9.

(Opposite and Right) Bold logs and wood-paned windows sit behind a fieldstone patio wall in an atmosphere of wood and lake serenity.

MINNESOTA LOG CABIN

OWNERS: Anonymous
ARCHITECTS: Meyer, Scherer & Rockcastle, Ltd., Thomas Meyer, AIA, Partner in Charge; Christine Albertsson, AIA, Project Architect
PHOTOGRAPHER: Peter Kerze

The clients purchased their lake property for its size and for the romantic, original forties boathouse down on the water's edge, with its own summer apartment above. The completed renovation resulted in several small cabins that explore the themes of the rustic log cabin. On this wooded slope, the design includes large-scale logs, deep overhangs, and fieldstone walls. Patios and pergolas in the plush green landscape form many intimate outdoor spaces that belie the airy and open interior of the small cabin.

One enters the cabin through a low vestibule that opens into a vaulted-and-beamed great room.

The living room, kitchen, and dining alcove share the central area with a large stone fireplace. The small 850-square-foot main cabin consists of the great room, with a master bedroom suite on one side, and a sun room off the other. The sun room is furnished in a Victorian manner: large stone floor tiles, wicker-and-wood furniture, high-paned vertical opened windows, and a floor-to-ceiling stone fireplace. Views of the surrounding lush landscape can be enjoyed from the sun room and adjoining porch.

The owners eschewed a multi-bedroom retreat and the large and well-equipped kitchen facilities that

are the mainstay for continuous guests and entertaining. They prefer more serene and personal activities. A one-room bunkhouse, which sleeps four, is found at the end of a series of terraces that connect it to a trellised pergola patio. Guests are self-sufficient with beds in the bunkhouse and their own kitchenette in the boathouse.

The cabin is stick-framed using conventional lumber. Large-scale logs, broad overhangs, and the extensive use of fieldstone walls, porches, and piers throughout the structures re-create an era and an ideal. This treasured place is a reminiscence and a contemplation of all log cabins on the lake.

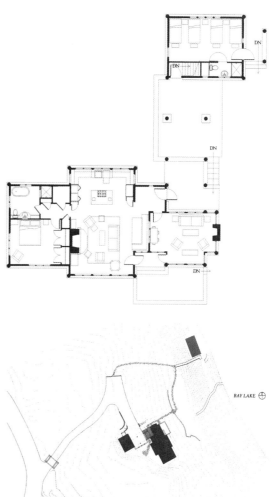

BAY LAKE

(Left) View up the path of main cabin in trees; to the right near the water is the boathouse with the kitchenette below for breakfast on the lake. *(Upper right)* A plan showing the main house with living room, sun room, and sleeping quarters connected by terraces to the bunkhouse. *(Lower right)* Site plan of main house, bunkhouse, and boathouse on the shore.

(Above) An informal living room and kitchen are made cozy with the use of a variety of woods in the flooring, cabinets, island, and ceiling. Local fieldstone is used in the broad and deep central fireplace. (Opposite) The full sun room features soft stone tiles and ceiling and walls of soft wood. A fieldstone fireplace and wood-paned windows come together to create a neo-Victorian atmosphere.

(*Opposite and Right*) This cabin is a retreat in the family orchard on one of the San Juan Islands.

Clam Shack

OWNERS: Anonymous
ARCHITECT: Sullivan Conard Architects
PHOTOGRAPHER: Steve Horn

An early-twentieth-century fishing camp occupied this site for years. Over time many old cabins were lost, and during a winter storm in 1991, a fire inside this family's old cabin destroyed it. The owners wished to remain faithful to the vernacular of the camps and chose to build another small, simple cabin in the style of the neighboring and last surviving structure in the compound.

The revival cabin is on the water's edge near Deer Harbor on Orcas Island in the San Juan Islands, north of Puget Sound. The cabin sits among trees that once belonged to an orchard. It faces south toward the sea in a secretive and personal landscape. The sounds of the Sound ripple through open doors and windows; the trees become individuals in the field. A strong chimney and terrace, constructed of local stone, anchor the cabin to the island terrain. The exterior is clad in indigenous cedar shingles that surround the well-planned, intermittent paned windows and French doors. It was designed as a place for guests, one that looked as though it had existed on the site for a century. It was to insinuate itself into the landscape, rather than come alive only when people came and went summer after summer.

The cabin interior is small, one thousand square feet, but soft and inviting. The walls and ceilings of white pine are reminiscent of Swedish *lusthaus* interiors, where light is honored above everything else. The broad and tall stone fireplace is the focal point of the main room; a bay window with a cushioned banquette conserves space in the light-filled dining alcove. A master bedroom and a child's bunk are fitted into the compact design and generously accommodate the whole family in this historic and pristine island setting.

(Upper left) The master bedroom is clad in light soft wood. The French doors open into the orchard, filling the room with the oxygen-rich air of these islands in the Northwest. (Upper right) The Clam Shack has a need for a compact and efficient kitchen. (Left) The children's bunk room can sleep six. The white pine throughout keeps the interior bright and cheery. (Opposite) The central living space includes the large fireplace and a built-in nook for half of the dining seating.

(*Opposite and Right*) The cabin was built as an homage to a childhood on the farm.

TEW BARN

OWNERS: John and Susan Tew
ARCHITECTS: Historical Concepts, LLP;
Design Team: James Strickland, Terry Pylant, David Bryant, Jeff Morrison, and Philip Windsor
PHOTOGRAPHER: Richard Leo Johnson

John and Susan Tew wanted to design a retreat that was reminiscent in style and feeling to John's childhood on a farm. The Spring Island, South Carolina, cabin is built in the vernacular form of farm buildings; theirs most resembles a country barn. The entire structure is constructed of reclaimed lumber, including authentic step treads worn from years of use. Cedar logs are used for the exterior decking. A timber-framed, screened porch provides open views of the island salt marshes beyond the barn.

The design evolved to its present state with the entertainment and activity spaces on the first floor and the daily living spaces on the upper level. The lower level was initially used as a storage facility. Over time, the owners modified the space to include a game room, as well as provide instant "al fresco" parties by opening all the barn doors.

The upper level has a great room, encompassing a compact kitchen, dining area, and seating. In this upper living space, the clients were able to influence the design team enough to create sleeping space for eight in an area of less than nine hundred square feet. A loft above the kitchenette is a small sleeping area. A bunk room with two built-in bunks off the great room has a sliding barn door to create privacy.

A unique use of shuttering includes long overhangs, which provide cooling shadows but prevent shutters from opening and closing. In order to incorporate shutters into the design, the team placed them on a track and they simply slide back and forth, out of the way of the overhangs. In the large gable, the track is designed to allow the shutters to slide down and out at a forty-five-degree angle, using counterweights and a pulley, to clear the roof line.

Inside and out, the overall character and emotion of the Tew barn is an era and a world away from today.

(Left) Galvanized metal roof covers the nine hundred square feet of interior space. A screened, timber-framed porch at the rear of the cabin provides views to the marshes beyond. *(Above)* An open-air porch is tucked under the screened porch above. Wooden rockers on wood planks, a table set with wildflowers, and the sound of birdsong emanating from the trees make a perfect day.

(Above) The bunk room, just off the great room, features two built-in bunks. (Left) The bunk room features a sliding barn door. (Opposite) The living, dining, and kitchen space is governed by a unique light fixture designed to enhance the tree house and barn appeal of the cabin. Hung from the corners of the skylights to a height below the beams, it is made of old rope and four antique globes and is a unifying element in the overall design.

(*Opposite and Right*) A gentle burst of forms and angles accommodates the varied activities of the family at the Texas lake.

HIGHLAND LAKE HOUSE

OWNERS: Anonymous
ARCHITECT: Lake | Flato Architects; Karla Greer, Project Architect
PHOTOGRAPHER: Timothy Hursley

On the shoreline of lovely LBJ Lake in central Texas is a special place to relax on weekends. The owners of the Highland Lake House asked their architect to design a vacation home for the immediate family. The design focused on the need for privacy, lots of fresh air and continuous ventilation, a variety of indoor and outdoor experiences, and wonderful interaction with the lake itself.

A flat, grassy playing field skirts the structures and connects two distinct one-story buildings that follow the point of land into the lake. The main house is entered at an intermediate level with stairs that descend into a large central room that rises to a glass cupola above. Exposed concrete floors at the ground level keep the circulating air cool and require very little maintenance. Large swinging and pocket-screen doors open a substantial section of the wall to the porch, which overlooks the lake below. What appear to be very thick walls house two guest rooms and a bath, which are arranged in a Pullman-car fashion with windows that overlook the center living space. Below, the thick wall creates a dining area which is open to the kitchen. The screened pavilion is an all-season room where friends and family gather to enjoy activities.

A boardwalk runs along the shoreline, eventually leading to a private pier and the boathouse. Back up at the street level, a breezeway becomes an open path through to the lake, connecting two additional guest rooms that sit on large wooden piers above the lake. The breezeway can be closed off with a large, sliding barn-type door that provides privacy and shelter from the wind.

All buildings have standing-seam, galvanized-metal roofs to complement the integral stucco-colored siding. The stucco is artfully carried into many of the interior walls and merges beautifully with the soft, whitewashed pine walls.

(Upper left) Upper-level bedroom interior is paneled in the white oak carried through from the dome of the great room below. (Upper right) A hall connects the rooms above the great room and a window opens onto the great room below. (Lower left) The great room includes a fireplace nook. (Opposite) A skylight seals the room and the windows indicate upper bedrooms connected by the long hall.

(Left) The large kitchen merges into an activity room. Stained concrete floors flow throughout the lower level of the house, keeping the circulating air cool. *(Above)* The lake winds around the small peninsula, creating continuous soft breezes through the covered porch.

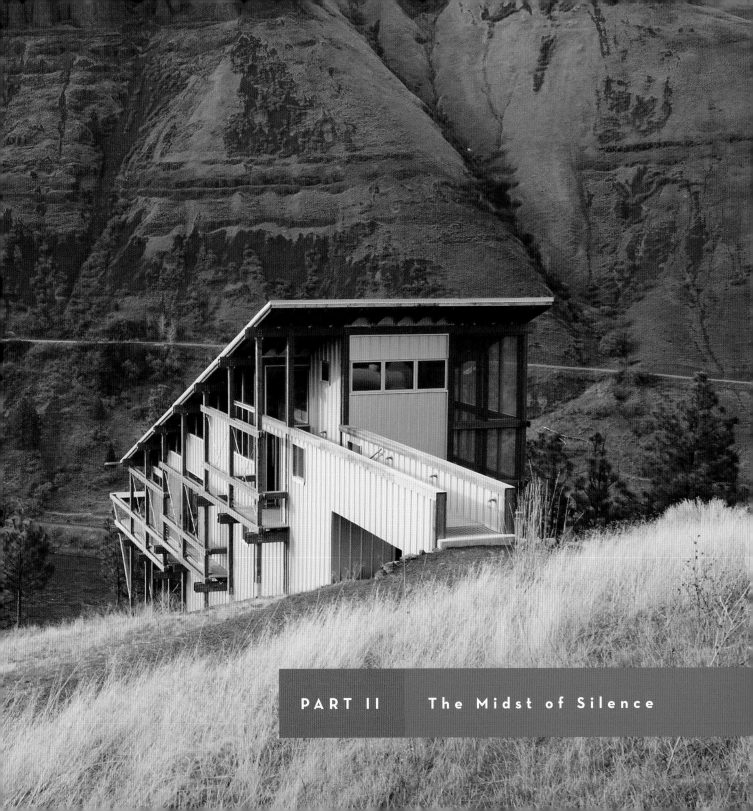

PART II   The Midst of Silence

(*Opposite and Right*) In the middle of a Michigan winter, the cabin is a refuge of comfort and warmth.

JOSIE'S CABIN

OWNERS: Bob and Josie Mossburg
ARCHITECTS: Robert B. Sears, Sears Architects; Rob Mossburg, Owner, The Cottage Company of Harbor Springs
PHOTOGRAPHER: Dave Speckman, Don Rutt Photography

Josie's cabin is located on a heavily wooded hundred-acre site five miles north of Harbor Spring, Michigan. This part of the country provides a feast for the soul during each and every season: Spring is filled with hidden morels and trilliums whose blossoms look as though fresh snow had fallen. Summers bring lush ferns and other greenery—a stark contrast to the white sandy beach and thrillingly blue waters of the Lake Michigan shoreline. Autumn is Josie Mossburg's favorite time of year. Its unmatched calico of colors, warm days, cool nights, and a promise of winter festivities and a spring certain to come, is embedded in the earth and air. And winter, finally winter, with its solitude and silent beauty—its warm and welcoming glow in the freezing night sky.

Josie's cabin is surrounded by a landscape that is home to many species of wildlife, whose welfare is of great concern to the Mossburgs. They have put a conservation easement on their property which will permanently protect a large portion of the land. The cabin was built as a gift for Josie by her son, Rob, and her husband, Bob. The design was intended to exhibit roots based in northern Michigan's vernacular log architecture: beginning as a place with humble origins, perhaps a one-room cabin, with additions that allowed for new and extra room, over time. This is where the Mossburgs wanted to gather with their visiting children and grandchildren. Thus the interior features an open floor plan with random-width oak planking. Plenty of windows keep the interior filled with natural light. A large and broad screened porch and outdoor fireplace extend activity areas. The families love to spend time on the porch grilling many meals year-round. The half-log exterior and interior is combined with 2" x 2" boards to serve as chinking, giving the cabin its wonderland glow.

(*Above*) The large stone fireplace inside the enclosed wraparound porch offers instant comfort for all. (*Right*) The interior great room includes the kitchen and island, and dining and living areas. A fieldstone fireplace and log and chinking become a refined backdrop for Josie's choice of interior furnishings.

(Upper left) The dining area is set into a bay of oversized windows; the beamed ceiling with a chandelier creates a lovely rustic elegance. (Lower left) Snow on the bedroom balcony reflects its own brightness on the beadboard ceiling of the upstairs bedroom. (Opposite) There couldn't be a more welcoming sight.

(*Opposite and Right*) The moss and rock garden is an extension of the serenity of the cabin. The exterior is dark gray cement board. An L-shaped wall of galvanized steel encloses the cabin and the garden.

Camano Island Cabin

OWNER: Karin Venator
ARCHITECT: Tim Carlander, Vandeventer & Carlander Architects
PHOTOGRAPHER: Steve Keating, Steve Keating Photography

Island life is spectacular in many ways, not the least of which is the forever changing seascape. This cabin is on a high bluff of island waterfront with southwestern views across Saratoga Passage and the Olympic Mountain Range in Washington. Long and narrow, the site is accessible from the county road at the crest of the property. A drive winds down through a dense thicket of evergreens, opening at the cabin and the glory of Puget Sound. A final hairpin turn brings the drive to the cabin and garden, located on a low-sloped bench of land roughly one hundred yards from the bluff.

The owners split their time between the cabin and their forty-eight-foot sailboat, *Ahti* (the Finnish god of the sea), which is moored in Semiahmoo, Washington. When they are not sailing in the Straits of San Juan de Fuca and Georgia, and around the Gulf Islands, they are happy to be at the cabin tending a precious garden. The design goals of the cabin were privacy, natural light, and an openness between indoors and outdoors, all packaged within an easily constructed building. The solution was a simple wood-frame box, topped with a sloped shed roof that accommodates a sleeping loft. An exterior landscape wall was built of galvanized steel to wrap around the diminutive moss and rock garden.

The cabin is an open volume: under the loft is a small kitchen. The main living area has two large sets of glazed doors that open south to the enclosed garden and west to the Sound. The owners became their own general contractors and finish carpenters. The exterior is finished with fiber-cement panels. A metal-clad wall creates a backdrop.

The interior is finished with a stained concrete slab floor on the main level and cherry-strip flooring in the loft. Walls and ceilings are finished in maple and cherry plywoods. The cabin is 352 square feet of elegance and flair, a perfect expression of understanding one's land-based needs and desires.

(Opposite) The interior is compact and efficient. A sleeping loft with a clerestory sits above the kitchen and bath areas, adding natural light to the living room. *(Upper left)* A ship's ladder leads to the sleeping loft. The doors open a large section of the wall to extraordinary views. *(Above)* The sleeping loft is exquisite in finish and detail. *(Lower left)* The living room ends with a wood stove and opens to the enclosed evergreen, stone, and moss garden.

(*Above*) The use of steel and cement
board materials are a counterpoint to the
setting, as well as a way of emphasizing
the natural surroundings. (*Right*) The
cabin, garden, and site.

(Opposite) The bridge to the cabin, which overlooks the Clearwater River in Idaho. *(Right)* The studio path goes up-slope to the canyon house.

CANYON CABIN

OWNERS: Kenneth and Jean Campbell
ARCHITECT: Paul F. Hirzel
PHOTOGRAPHER: Art Grice

Ten miles upstream from Lewiston, Idaho, is a wilderness retreat unlike any other. On forty acres of southern canyon-side land overlooking the Clearwater River is a two-building getaway where life is vivid and thoughts of university teaching and the law office fade quickly. The Campbells asked their architect for a design that would help them "cultivate the spiritual aspects in the trinity of human, fish, and river."

The "cabin" is actually two cabins: "the bunkhouse" is settled into a ravine along a seasonal stream; the "studio house" is perched on a finger ridge where a slope of bunch grass and Idaho fescue meet a ponderosa pine forest about three-hundred feet above the Clearwater River. A third destination is a perfectly shaped basalt knoll with a commanding observation point overlooking the canyon, which was preserved as an "outside place." The location of the studio house was determined by the location of the best fish sightings. In Ken Campbell's words, it was sited "to mark the holding spot of steelhead for two-hundred yards in the fishy looking run along the river's south bank."

The studio is a rectangular form anchored onto the hillside. A bridge extension provides access to a path that goes to the bunkhouse. The west side of the cabin is a *brise-soleil* that allows for easy window washing and is a support for removal of perforated sliding panels—for shading and wind protection. On the east side, the frame supports decks and a screened porch with an outdoor shower. Operable windows on all four sides of the cabin allow natural updraft ventilation as summer temperatures in the canyon often exceed one hundred degrees Fahrenheit. Windstorms often blast through the canyon, gusting at seventy miles per hour.

The bunkhouse is a place of refuge. Tucked into the folds of a ravine about three hundred yards from the studio, its east and west façades are punctuated with windows that offer views of different micro-environments. A rock fall, a hawthorne thicket, vivid bird life, and the river below all occupy each frame. This is a perfect place to write, sleep, talk, eat, read, fish, cleanse, garden, and wander.

(Right) This year-round retreat was created with utilitarian materials: The interior floors are galvanized steel diamond plate and oriented strand board. Douglas fir was used for framing and Idaho white pine for walls and cabinetry. *(Lower left)* The stair descends from the upper-level loft to the dining level, and down to the living room level. Materials were chosen to provide hardiness to the challenges of the severe climate. *(Opposite)* The lower living area offers a wood stove and built-in wood niches.

(Left) Perched on a finger ridge, the studio house is about three-hundred feet above the Clearwater River. The studio house is subject to extreme exposure, which called for a brise-soleil to accommodate removable, perforated sliding panels from high gusting winds and one-hundred-degree temperatures. (Above) The bunkhouse is tucked into the folds of a ravine, about three-hundred yards from the studio house.

(*Opposite and Right*) A stone path winds through the bare trees to this jewel in the winter woods.

OHIO CABIN

OWNER: Thoa Kim Tran
ARCHITECT: Jeffrey L. Zucker, AIA, Zucker Architecture
PHOTOGRAPHER: David Steinbrunner

There is nothing comparable to the flash of excitement that ripples through the veins when a morel makes itself visible under the mulch of last autumn's leaves in the heart of the forest. Perhaps, wandering through the hills of southern Ohio, stumbling upon this magical mystery house deep in the forest, one might experience a similar feeling. The stone cabin itself resembles nothing so much as a cluster of fungi hanging from the side of a tree. A stone

base and organic roof make the building seem invisible. In the mists made by the nearby river bottoms, the cabin virtually disappears into the shadows.

Architect Jeffrey Zucker apprentices under Paolo Soleri at Arcosanti in Arizona. It is surprising that one of his first solo projects would be in the Ohio landscape; however, he managed to incorporate many efficient design elements into this temperate-climate home. The cabin,

begun in 1976, is a passive-solar structure utilizing lots of circles in its design. The roof is literally draped from the mast of the chimney, over the circular spaces, and lifted around the perimeters. The results are cresent-shaped windows with heavy brows.

The Stone House is a celebration of energy independence and also of the practical use of recycled materials. Much of the wood used on the warm interior spaces was

gleaned from nearby saw mills; the stone was gathered from surrounding creeks. The rooms gradually wind around the central core, nautiluslike, with heat rising and emanating from the massive Russian fireplace in the lower-level living room. The fireplace rises to warm the bath and shower area, which is a few steps from the master bedroom. A hidden door near the shower opens to the outside for toweling off on a beautiful summer day.

When Jeff returned to Arizona to open his architectural practice, he turned the house over to trusted friend and contractor, Jack Vetter. Jack successfully completed Jeff's design. Today, the Stone House lives in the forest, as much a part of nature as its neighboring morels and trees.

(*Opposite*) The bath and shower stones are warmed by the fireplace behind them. The bath is steps from the master bedroom. (*Upper left*) A hallway leads to the bedroom. (*Upper right*) The bedroom features a sunken bath and shower, as rooms rise and wrap nautiluslike around the central fireplace.

(*Opposite and Right*) This cabin is 186 square feet of Colorado getaway.

SMITH MCLAIN CABIN

OWNERS: James C. Smith and Deborah J. McLain
ARCHITECT: James C. Smith, Smiths
PHOTOGRAPHERS: Robin T. Smith, Cheryl Unger, and Hal Stoelzle

This remote Colorado cabin is a long drive from the nearest small town, Cotopaxi, and a three-hour drive from Denver. The landscape is diverse; terrain luxuriates between open meadows, aspen groves, and sprinklings of windblown bristlecone and limber pines on rolling hills and rocky outcroppings. The cabin sits atop a rocky knoll at a ninety-eight-hundred-foot elevation, with an unobstructed view of the entire Sangre De Cristo Mountain Range. This exquisite spine of mountains is often compared to a child's drawing for its simple clarity of form.

As a project, the 186-square-foot cabin represents the need for two urban dwellers to escape the city. In a subdivided cattle ranch of forty-acre plots, the cabin is a modern day settler's claim. The cabin's skin is alternately tongue-and-groove cedar and 5/8" exterior plywood with 1" x 4" cedar slating over 2" x 2" battens. The design recalls the horizontal lines in the body of settlers' cabins and the vertical quality of board and batten frequently used in the gable. Battens are installed directly behind 2" x 4" studs concealing plywood joints and linking vertically to the roof joists. This configuration reveals the inner construction of studs that are spaced at 16" on center. The screen provides security shutters over windows and an escape from the heat of the midday sun.

Varying pitches and attenuated extensions of the roof recall the bristlecone as it responds to the wind. The differing heights create a hierarchy of space between the kitchen and mudroom areas and the living area. Galvanized corrugated-metal roofing and details both inside and out assure longevity and are a link to the indigenous vocabulary of "ranch."

The owners associate an almost spiritual sense with the experience of being at the cabin. The brightness of the stars, the silence, and the rawness of the environment are the perfect counterpoint to days in the city. Reading, playing Scrabble by kerosene light, and cooking "great makeshift meals" on a small propane stove are part of the lure. Hiking on old carriage roads that pass homesteads and decaying log cabins or ice skating and playing hockey on a frozen cattle pond are more than enough to look forward to. Summer or winter, the cabin has a remarkable ability to rebuild one's connection to the earth.

(Left) The opened French doors reveal the cabin's interior, including a compact living area with a kitchen and a wood stove. (Upper right) A farmer's sink and propane stove are almost luxuries at the 9,800-foot elevation. Here, meals take on an air of sacred grace. (Opposite) The cabin, shown here with its window shutters and French doors open, features a corrugated metal roof.

(Opposite and Right) This cabin was designed with farm and ranch vernacular architecture in mind. The setting, free of clutter, is beside a serene pond; the house is the picture of calm.

Von Blon Retreat

OWNERS: Phillip and Joanne Von Blon
ARCHITECTS: Meyer, Sherer & Rockcastle, Ltd.
Thomas Meyer, Principal in Charge; Barry Petit, Project Manager; Greg Abnet, Project Architect
PHOTOGRAPHERS: George Heinrich, Lea Babcock Scherer

The essence of this cabin is expressed in each detail. Inside or out, serenity, attentiveness, and intensified silences permeate the air. Phillip and Joanne Von Blon are a busy and productive couple who entertain frequently, collect art and artifacts, and practice t'ai chi. On ninety acres of woodland and prairie grass, reflected in a large pond, this building is meant to convey a glimpse of a rural American vernacular found in nineteenth- and early-twentieth-century farm- and-ranch structures. Vernacular buildings are designed and built by the people who use them, and they evolve with the needs of the people who live and work in and around them. Here, a central single-volume living area is surrounded by "lean-to" additions, which house the private areas. A rectangular stone foundation surrounds the entire structure to establish the domain of the house and an edge between the cultivated outdoor space and the wildness of the prairie.

A second aspect of the design takes inspiration from the site. Two outdoor corner areas within the stone foundation reflect individual orientations and views. The southwest-facing sunny corner overlooks the calming glass-surfaced pond, which was created in a clearing in the woods. This wood-decked corner contains a small flower garden, a screened porch, and the entry porch. The northwest-facing cool corner is located on the crest of a long gently sloping hillside and has views of miles and miles of the local countryside. In the cool corner of the property is a folly of ruins. It is not only a place of quiet contemplation but a sculpture among soft grass, smooth rocks, and soothing perennials. Orientation of the dwelling and its interior spaces has an influential bearing on the harmony of living and spending time here.

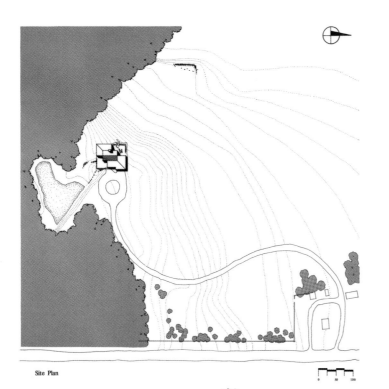

Site Plan

0   50   100

Section Looking South

0 1   5   10

Section Looking West

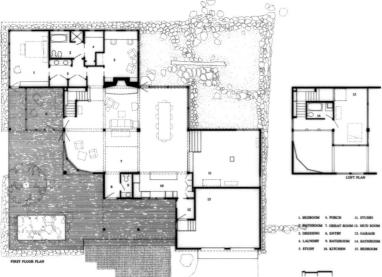

FIRST FLOOR PLAN

LOFT PLAN

1. BEDROOM   6. PORCH   11. STUDIO
2. BATHROOM   7. GREAT ROOM 12. MUD ROOM
3. DRESSING   8. ENTRY   13. GARAGE
4. LAUNDRY   9. BATHROOM   14. BATHROOM
5. STUDY   10. KITCHEN   15. BEDROOM

(Upper left) Site plan showing winding road to cabin and pond near woods. *(Upper right)* Section looking south *(top)*; Section looking west *(bottom)*. *(Lower left)* Plan and legend for cabin and loft space. *(Opposite)* View of cabin with "added" spaces and "lean-to" structures.

(*Opposite*) View from the t'ai chi practice room into the dining space and reading nook. Kitchen is on left. (*Upper left*) Living area with wall of stone and fireplace. Stair leads to loft overhead. (*Upper right*) Entry to great room.

FOREST GUEST CABIN

OWNERS: Anonymous
ARCHITECTS: Meyer, Sherer & Rockcastle, Ltd.
Thomas Meyer AIA, Principal in Charge
Bill Huntress, AIA, Project Manager
Mark Reckin, Project Designer
PHOTOGRAPHER: Peter Kerze

(*Opposite*) Horizontal and vertical planes dominate the prairie and treed landscape. Flat stone is also part of the surrounding area. Design echoes landscape and materials. (*Above*) Built walls and forms accentuate the natural landscape.

Educated as a modernist architect, now the mother of three young girls, this owner designed the family guesthouse with all of the romance, warmth, compatibility, and familiarity of a traditional stone-and-timber structure. This building is perfectly adapted to its own unique and contemporary setting. Here is found the old and the new, the romantic and the authentic, myths and ideas. The eighteen-acre site was chosen at the literal edge of a woods where a reclaimed prairie begins. The two distinct environments offer two views of the natural world. The design evolves from an interaction between the agricultural legacy of the site's fields and fence rows, and

two new stone walls. Located in the open prairie portion of the site, one of the two new walls anchors the horizontal main house, while the other wall—on the forest part of the site—anchors the more vertical guest cabin. The stone wall alongside the building defines this edge and extends out into the site, shaping the area of arrival and entry, emphasizing the woods and prairie polarity.

The building is itself designed as a two-part composition: one is the quintessential long and low "prairie" form; the other, a two-story-tall slender volume, a "woods" structure. The low stone wall that anchors the prairie shape erodes into the land at each end of the wall. The tower has

a slight twist and "leans" as it ascends into the treetops.

The interior first floor is an open great room that includes the kitchen, eating area, living area, and screened porch. Along an interior stone wall on the second level which is punctuated with windows and overhead lighting, are bookshelves and cabinets under an open-beam ceiling. The other half of the room is clad in local virgin pine salvaged from old industrial buildings. The vertical volume that rises through the trees houses two built-in sleeping areas— one for kids and one for parents. The intersecting planes and volume offer a strong abstraction of the woods and prairie landscape outside.

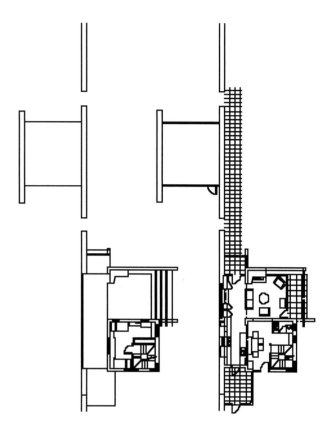

(*Upper left*) Lower-level entry to great room, kitchen on left. The large post- and beam treatment is combined with detailed cabinetry and a dark parquet floor. (*Upper right*) Floor plans (*Lower right and Lower left*) Site plans (*Opposite*) Second level is shown with open beams and a long stone wall with built-in cabinetry in the horizontal design.

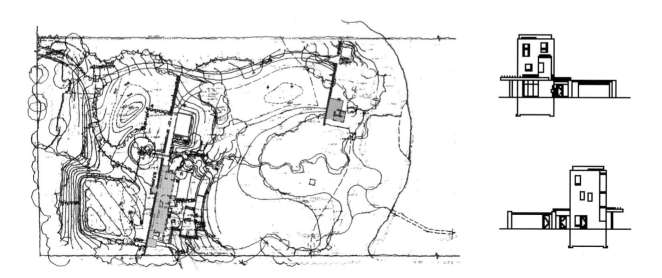

(*Above*) Horizontal planes disappear into landscape. Vertical volume makes its presence and intrigue known. (*Right*) Beautifully stacked thin fieldstone extends the horizontal lines. Window framing is deeply set into the stone. (*Opposite*) Vertical volume is supported by stone and reaches the tops of the trees. The small balcony projects, "branch-like" into the air from a bedroom.

PART III   Having a Hand in the Seasons

(Opposite and Right) Weightlessness, mass, and voids float solidly among wild-flowers for a refreshing getaway retreat.

STEPHENTOWN CABIN

OWNERS: Anonymous
ARCHITECT: David J. Weiner; David J. Weiner, Architect, P.C.
PHOTOGRAPHER: Tony Morgan, Step Graphics, Inc.

At twelve-hundred square feet, this weekend getaway is a large flower in the seven-acre meadow where it sits. The hilltop property overlooks the Berkshire Mountains with the meadow sloping to the south. The client requested that the dwelling have a compactness and an interior aesthetic spareness akin to traditional Japanese architecture.

The building is conceived as a single sweeping volumetric "sheet" that wraps and folds into itself, while at the same time giving definition to two distinct and major interior spaces. The primary interior space is used for cooking, dining, and living. An extended, closed-in, porchlike aperture is comparable to what is known as an *engawa*, or an "in-between space," which is found in Japanese architecture. The *engawa* in this design extends off the main space to frame the primary views. It is perceived as a "leaving" of one place and an "entering" of another between the interior and the exterior. The *engawa* ties the building and the lap pool to the landscape.

The secondary interior space serves as the master-bedroom suite. The house is designed for economy of construction and of maintenance. Painted gypsum board and wood-paneled interior partitions, a membrane roof, and a wood-frame construction, with tongue-and-groove exterior cedar siding, helped to keep costs low.

The site has been untouched and parts have been renaturalized to encourage the growth of wildflowers in the surrounding meadow.

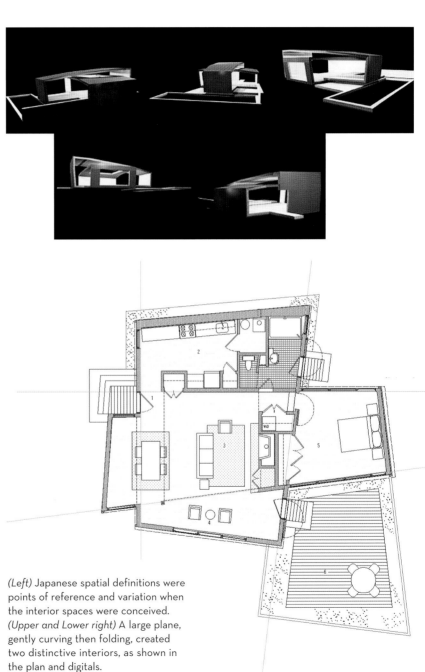

(Left) Japanese spatial definitions were points of reference and variation when the interior spaces were conceived. *(Upper and Lower right)* A large plane, gently curving then folding, created two distinctive interiors, as shown in the plan and digitals.

(Upper left) The master suite floats in a peaceful realm of air and greenery at the narrow and streamlined end of the retreat. *(Lower left)* The living space in the great room faces in the direction of the master suite, where the clerestory nears its highest volume. *(Lower right)* Behind the living area is the dining room. From the dining area, steps lead to a wine cellar. *(Opposite)* Artificial light fills the entire interior volume at dusk.

(Opposite and Right) Summer grasses and the sod roof make this classic retreat above the fog irresistible. Thanks to the inspired architecture, the structure cools and heats itself all year long.

CROWELL HOUSE

OWNERS: Joan and David Crowell
ARCHITECT: Mark Simon, FAIA, Centerbrook Architects and Planners
PHOTOGRAPHER: Oberto Gilli

The small vacation house for the architect's parents is set into the side of a large open hill. Grand vistas reach out to the Green Mountains of Vermont, which are forty miles away. The cabin has a deep sod roof with eighteen inches of earth on it that provides insulation and camouflages it from view from farther up the hillside.

The house is designed with passive solar heat. The only exposed wall faces southwest, taking in the sun's heat in the fall, winter, and spring. The porch roof provides shade in the summer and is built around a decorated gable that reassures nervous occupants that they are still in a house like those of the nearby farms and Victorian homesteads. The other three walls, set deep into the earth—which remain a steady fifty degrees even in the coldest of winters—are concrete and insulated by wall and earth. There is exceptional thermal momentum to store heat from day to night. The backup heating system consists of two wood stoves. During the first winter, a maximum/minimum thermometer showed that, unoccupied, the house never got colder than thirty-one degrees Fahrenheit inside, while outside, temperatures dipped to negative thirty-one degrees. The cabin stays cool and dry in summer with a vapor barrier and air pocket between the interior siding and the concrete walls, and with ventilation through the skylights.

Interior finishes in the sleeping alcove and throughout the cabin are of local wide-board white pine and exposed Douglas fir rafters set on 6" centers. Maple bobbins, manufactured nearby for cotton mills, are set into the walls like Shaker pegs to hold vacation detritus.

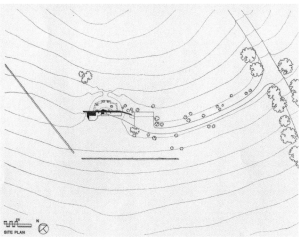

SITE PLAN

(*Above*) The kitchen, dining, and elevated sleeping or reading nook are shown here; the interior treatment is wide-board white pine. (*Opposite*) A double-duty space, where there is room for games, reading, or sleeping in warmth and comfort.

(Above) The central room leads to an extra space where the wood stove is used when necessary. (Upper right) White pine throughout lends a contemporary rusticity to the cabin. (Lower right) The wood-stove backup heating system. (Opposite) The cabin in several feet of snow. During the first winter, the cabin, unoccupied, never got colder than thirty-one degrees Fahrenheit inside, while outside, temperatures dipped to negative thirty-one degrees.

(Opposite and Right) The strength and power of the cabin design is a match for the extreme climate of the North Cascade Mountains.

NORTH CASCADES CABIN

OWNERS: Anonymous
ARCHITECT: Nils Finne, Finne Architects
BUILDER: Rick Mills
PHOTOGRAPHER: Art Grice

This cabin in Washington State's North Cascades is part of a continuing investigation into the lyrical qualities of wood and stone for architect Nils Finne. The site is located at the north end of a beautiful, pristine valley between a large open meadow and a dramatic mountain ridge. The meadow has a cross-country ski trail that is groomed during the winter, with links to other trails; when the cabin door is opened one is on the ski trail.

A series of complex wood trusses provides the major ordering element of the design. The trusses are sup-ported by stone walls of split-face Montana ledge stone. The roof line begins very steeply at the peak, then breaks into a gentle slope over the nine-foot-deep stone porch, which is continuous on both sides of the cabin. The deep roof overhangs express a strong sense of shelter and also of welcome.

High clerestory windows allow the interior to enjoy generous amounts of natural light. Additional high windows placed within dormers also allow natural ventilation during the hot summer months. The cabin is designed for both the cold, snow-laden winters, as well as for the hot, dry summer months. The broad porches provide protection from the heavy winter snows and are a wonderful, cool, shady place to sit during the summer.

The interior is a straightforward plan, with an open space containing areas for living and dining; cooking takes place at the east end of the cabin. The bedrooms and a loft are at the west end. The long face of the cabin is to the south. A dramatic steel-and-wood bridge to the children's loft passes over the kitchen and ends at a stair, close to the front

door, allowing movement to and from the loft—mostly by the children—to become a part of the main space and to be even slightly theatrical.

The major building materials are gorgeous Montana ledge stone for the exterior walls, and Douglas fir trusses, purlins, and interior wood panels. The exterior porches are stone; the interior floor is cast concrete with a custom veneer finish. The floors feature inlaid strips of stone mosaic. This Northern Cascades cabin will be in this family for many generations to come.

(Opposite) Bunks and built-ins make good use of available space in beautiful wood interiors. *(Right)* Sliding doors with frosted glass panes close easily and divide the bunk room from other areas. *(Lower left)* Attention to detail is a Finne Architects trademark. Stair design is by Nils Finne.

(Opposite and Right) Complex Douglas fir trusses are the major ordering element in the design.

(Opposite and Right) Stucco and steel settle lightly on the site. The cabin is anchored directly into the slope.

MAZAMA CABIN

OWNERS: Sharon Cupp and D. J. Jones
ARCHITECT: Thomas Lawrence; Lawrence Architecture
PHOTOGRAPHER: Benjamin Benschneider

Perched high above a river on a south-facing bluff on the eastern slope of the Cascade Mountains in eastern Washington State, this small cabin rests among the trees and opens out to expansive views of the Methow River and the mountains beyond. Designed as a simple box with a shed roof, the cabin sits lightly on a half acre of land with minimal impact on the surrounding landscape. Made of stucco, the uphill side of the cabin is set directly into the hillside and acts as an anchor for the rest of the structure. The downhill side is composed of corrugated-metal siding and large windows, elevated above the ground.

The one-bedroom, one-bath cabin is designed with kitchen and living areas, a loft space, extra sleeping space, and a ski-waxing room. The central area includes the "sleeping alcove" for visitors as well as a bay with built-in seating at the kitchen/dining table. The square footage is a surprising 820 square feet, with a 440-square-foot loft; exterior space expands the experience with a 145-square-foot entry porch and a 280-square-foot deck. The interiors are made to feel cozy and warm with bamboo flooring, veneer-and-plaster walls, and tongue-and-groove, wood-paneled ceilings.

(*Left*) A small wood stove heats the cabin interior. (*Below*) The view from the elevated sleeping platform through the cabin living room to the kitchen and breakfast nook. (*Opposite and Lower right*) Activity areas are easily defined with furnishings, nooks, and platforms. The ship's ladder leads to sleeping lofts above.

The interior expresses two components of the cabin's design. The solid stucco part of the cabin is comprised of a "band" of small spaces: a bedroom and closet, a bathroom, the entry and mudroom, a pantry, and a ski-waxing room. After passing through this "band," the cabin opens into the light, transparent main space with the kitchen and dining bay at one end, living space in the center, and a bed/seating alcove at the opposite end.

The space is two stories with large glazed windows that open into the trees and offer views in three directions. Acting as the ceiling for the smaller spaces of the cabin, the open loft hovers over the main space and wraps around to form the bed alcove below it.

A south-facing deck extends out from the main living area and connects the cabin to the landscape as it reaches out to the blue outlines of the mountains in the distance.

(Opposite and Left) The deck extends out to face south, reaching toward the afternoon sun and the mountains. The "punched-out" space of the dining nook can be seen on the deck. *(Upper right)* At dusk, the cabin lights up the hillside with its interior glow.

(Opposite and Right) The wood-framed rectangle of windows encloses the interior space under a simple roof and affords views in all directions.

BIRDING CABIN

OWNERS: Kraig and Kathy Kemper
ARCHITECT: Suyama Peterson Deguchi
PHOTOGRAPHER: David Story

In the spirit of a tent, this wooden platform is protected by a simple gable roof that serves as inspiration for the owners who are avid bird watchers. The cabin inhabits the edge of a meadow between woods and the Sound. The open gabled end of the cabin faces south toward the migratory routes of hundreds of species of birdlife. The plan of this refuge calls for a pool to be created with an end view of the structure. The pool will be an attraction for the birds and will cause the platform to appear as if it is cantilevered out over the water. This will bring observation closer and multiply the pleasures of watching the returning flocks year after year.

Large blocks of polished concrete form steps leading into the cabin and distinguish the movement from the natural to the man-made. Poured concrete columns hold the wood platform in place, off the ground, and continue upward to support the metal-clad roof. A wood grid defines the cabin's enclosure and is filled with materials of varying degrees of transparency: insect screening, glass, or tongue-and-groove cedar planks. Two screened porches flank the main living space and run the length of the cabin, much as the *engawa* found in Japanese residential architecture does. An inner perimeter of glass and sliding wood panels (which are similar to shoji screens) partition the main living area from the sleeping areas. Obsessive, Japanese, blind mortise-and-tenon joinery proliferates throughout the cabin. Intended only for fair-weather use, the cabin is uninsulated, revealing even more of the meticulous construction. Natural finishes on the hand-planed, salvaged cedar planks preserve the beauty of the wood and warm up this simple, but never austere structure.

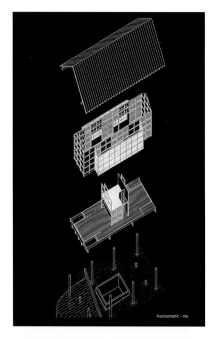

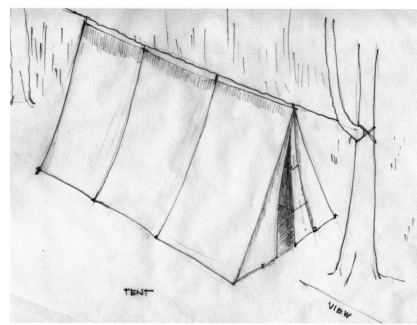

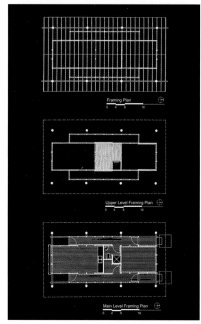

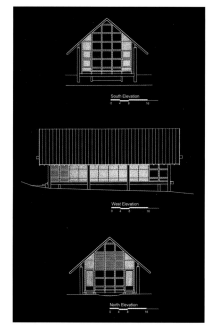

(Upper left) Exploded model of structure *(Upper right)* Sketch of simple tent *(Lower left)* Plans of each level *(Lower right)* South, West and North elevations *(Opposite)* The birding perch sits back against the trees with a full view of the migratory meadow and Puget Sound.

(*Opposite*) The center of the cabin is a small kitchen tucked under a sleeping loft. Fine joinery and exquisite simplicity define the interiors. (*Left*) A viewing room tucked into the other side of the two-level kitchen and loft looks back into the tree line. (*Above*) In fair weather the secluded room opens to face the tree-protected north side by means of a movable wall.

(Opposite and Right) This ski cabin is designed for extreme weather at a high altitude. The cabin faces south.

SUGAR BOWL

OWNERS: Anonymous
ARCHITECT: Mark Horton, Mark Horton Architecture
PHOTOGRAPHERS: Mark Horton, David Duncan Livingston

At a seven-thousand-foot elevation near Donner Summit, on a snow-bound slope of the Sierra Nevadas, this cabin is accessible only by skis or snowmobile during the winter. Sugar Bowl opened in 1939 with a lift up Mount Disney, the first chairlift in northern California. Noted architect William Wurster designed the Sugar Bowl Lodge, and it is still standing today. Wurster later went on to become the Dean of Architecture for Berkeley and M.I.T., and obviously knew how to build to withstand wind, weather, and time.

This weekend cabin was designed for an active San Francisco family in an area reputed to have the deepest snow load of any inhabited place in the continental United States. At the other end of the spectrum, the summers at Sugar Bowl can be extremely dry and hot, requiring a sensitive and direct design that responds to the wide-ranging environmental conditions. Mark Horton designed for the snow loads and heat extremes. A simple rectangular box is placed on a hillside with its open face to the south. The roof is pitched back to the north. A central design feature is the additional structure of the architectural "trees" that span from grade to roof on the interior. These structural columns branch out to support the ceiling. The design is inverted with the public space on the top level and the bunk rooms on the lower level.

The top level consists of the living room, dining room, a customized reading nook, cooking and breakfast areas. The placement of these areas raises them out of the normal twelve-foot-deep snow accumulation and brings them up into a viewing position in one uninterrupted space along the south side. Sauna, playroom, and TV room, along with a gym, bunk rooms, and baths, are on the lower level. A bright and open atrium connects all levels.

(Far left) Strong design elements bear the loads in the rectangular form of the cabin. The architect used "trees" that span from grade to roof for support in an area with massive snow loads. (Left) The delicate "trees" and the massive concrete fireplace mediate the interior with light and strength around elevated dining area. (Below) A concrete wall fireplace and hearth in the bedroom.

(*Left*) The large fireplace projects onto the small balcony from the living room.
(*Below*) At the rear of the cabin, the roof is designed to let snow fall downslope.
(*Opposite*) The front face of the cabin showing snow accumulation building below deck.

(Opposite) Cabin sits above a sandy beach reached by stone step pathway. *(Right)* Window wall opens to terrace and spa.

CHICKEN POINT

OWNER: Jeff Larson
ARCHITECT: Olson Sundberg Kundig Allen Architects
PHOTOGRAPHERS: Undine Prohl, Benjamin Benschneider, Mark Darley

The idea for the cabin was to create a lakeside shelter in the woods—a little box with a big window that opened to the surrounding landscape. The cabin's big window wall, which is thirty feet by twenty feet, opens the entire living space to the forest and to the lake. At twenty-six hundred square feet, the cabin is large enough to handle the family functions it was designed for, yet intimate enough to preserve its essential charm.

The cabin design called for three component parts: a concrete-block box, a plywood insert, and a four-foot-diameter steel fireplace affectionately named, "The Bong." The materials—concrete blocks, steel, concrete floors, and plywood—are very low maintenance, in keeping with the notion of a cabin. Left unfinished to age naturally and acquire a patina, the structure will blend with the surrounding idyllic setting. Open interior spaces are intended to be a seamless extension of the outdoors. The concrete floor inside extends outside to become part of the terrace and built-in spa.

A nineteen-foot-tall steel entry door is exaggerated in height to easily accommodate long skis. Once inside, the concrete-block volume is punctuated by relatively few distractions: a steel fireplace, a bridge that spans the main space, and the master sleeping alcove that floats above the kitchen area below. The cabin easily sleeps ten and is a playground for kids and adults. The six-ton window wall pivots on an off-center axis, its speed regulated by a fly-ball governor, "The Gizmo."

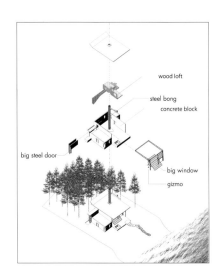

wood loft

steel bong

concrete block

big steel door

big window

gizmo

(Upper left) Exploded plan and site plan. (Upper right) Section. (Lower left) First-floor plan. (Lower right) Second floor and loft plan. (Opposite, upper left) The kitchen is tucked under the overhead sleeping loft. A table stabilized by steel coil offers seating for ten. (Opposite, upper right) Loft landing. (Opposite, lower left) The central forty-eight-inch-diameter steel floor-to-roof fireplace recalls an early seventies design by architect Paul Schweikher for his desert home in Arizona. (Opposite, lower right) The upper-level sleeping loft has views of the mountains and lake.

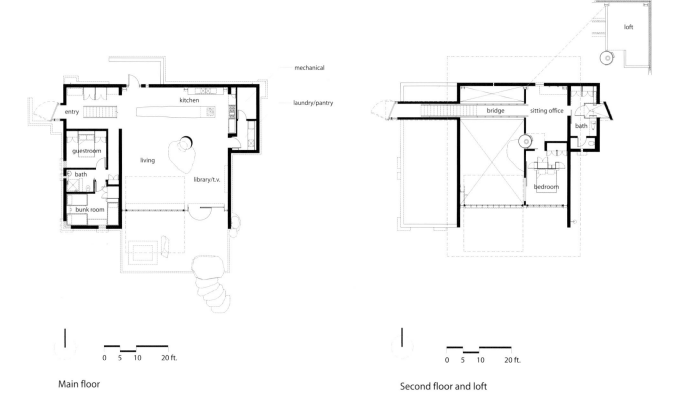

mechanical

laundry/pantry

entry

kitchen

guestroom

living

bath

library/t.v.

bunk room

Main floor

0 5 10   20 ft.

loft

bridge   sitting office

bath

bedroom

Second floor and loft

0 5 10   20 ft.

(Above) Looking toward the interior, over
the spa, the window walls are open.
(Right) The steel-framed and -paned window wall opens for full integration of
cabin living into the lake and outdoor
activities. (Following spread) Simple
materials, simple planes, and volumes
are used to create the cabin. (Following
spread right) Stairs leading to upper-
level loft.

(*Left*) Bunks with handy floor-to-ceiling shelving and storage; utility reading lights. (*Opposite*) Full enjoyment of an evening at Chicken Point. Steps to the lake and chairs on the beach.

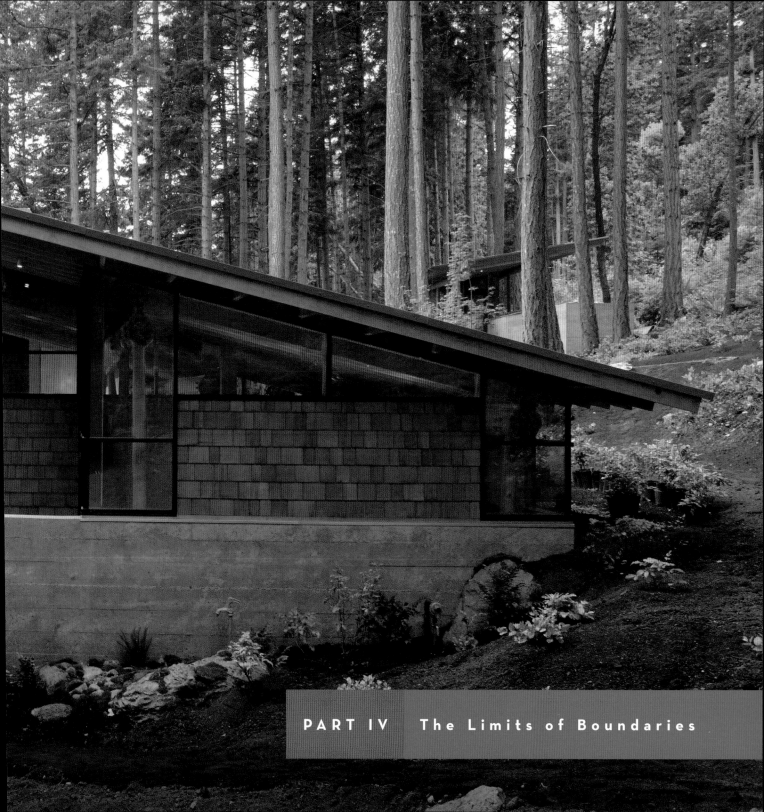

PART IV　The Limits of Boundaries

(Opposite) Emphatic geometry, hidden calculus, and plenty of open space are trademarks of Olle Lundberg design. *(Right)* A protective enclosure ensures that Mary Breuer's garden is heavy with tomatoes, salad greens, vegetables, and flowers.

SONOMA COUNTRY CABIN

OWNERS: Mary Breuer and T. Olle Lundberg
ARCHITECT: T. Olle Lundberg, AIA, Lundberg Design
PHOTOGRAPHER: Jon D. Peterson

A Sonoma County hillside is the perfect location for a few days away from the office in San Francisco. Architect Olle Lundberg never fails to mix the unanticipated, the beautiful, and the refreshing into his designs. Olle and Mary's cabin is on sixteen acres of redwood forest facing northeast over a pristine river canyon. The site and the cabin design are all about the view and the house opens up toward it. The deck projects itself and its guests out into the air, and the pool is the magic touch, allowing bathers the ultimate luxury of swimming twenty feet in the air—literally "in the treetops."

The main level of the cabin is 900 square feet with a 150-square-foot bedroom loft overlooking the living room and the distant valley. A large 1,500-square-foot deck runs from back to front along one side of the cabin, enclosing a spa and the twenty-five-foot-diameter swimming pool. This extraordinary feature—typical of Lundberg's playfulness—is a reclaimed redwood water tank that is fourteen feet deep. The tank is built into the hillside and is structurally supportive of the deck and cabin.

The exterior siding is redwood, the roof is standing seam copper, and all of the windows are reclaimed from remodeled buildings. The main floor is Chinese slate and the bedroom floor is maple. The kitchen cabinets are steel file cabinets on coasters for easy cleaning and mouse-proofing. The kitchen island, the dining table, which is made from a single slab of redwood, and the circular-steel firewood holder were designed and fabricated by Olle's firm, Lundberg Design.

Behind the cabin is a fenced vegetable garden occupying three thousand square feet. Mary tends the garden, which produces lush vegetables and "glorious" tomatoes each year. Just to get to the garden every weekend is Mary and Olle's "weekly dose of sanity."

(Upper left) A broad sweep of Chinese slate tiles are used throughout the main cabin level. The brushed stainless steel kitchen island and appliances have a utilitarian—and festive—look. *(Lower right)* The dining table is steps from the kitchen, tucked under the sleeping loft. Outside, the deck extends into the treetops. *(Opposite)* Attractive glass panels create the illusion that the living room is floating in the trees. The absence of a deck accentuates the drop-off from the bottom of the window. The wood-storage "wheel" was designed by T. Olle Lundberg.

(*Opposite*) An irresistible plunge: the swimming pool made from a reclaimed redwood water-tower tank. The depth is fourteen feet; its diameter is twenty-five feet. The tank is anchored into the side of the slope and offers structural support to the fifteen-hundred-square-foot deck. (*Upper left*) Walkways connect the entry, side and front decks, and garden. The plane of the shed roof is altered by a clerestory. (*Upper right*) Entry details: The wood-storage receptacle and outdoor sconce were designed by T. Olle Lundberg. (*Lower left*) The length of the deck including spa and pool.

(*Opposite*) Large sliding doors on each side of the great room create a see-through design; they open to decks for convenient dining and entertaining. (*Right*) A sumptuous evening in a remote and wild mountain landscape.

CARLISLE CABIN

OWNER: Tom Carlisle
ARCHITECT: Marley + Wells Architects
PHOTOGRAPHER: Tim Maloney, Technical Imagery Studios

In a remote area of the coastal mountains west of Healdsburg, California, Tom Carlisle dreamed of experiencing a bit of refined modern architecture in a natural, even wild landscape. The architect was confronted with numerous constraints and restrictions for designing and building in the area, not the least of which is the ever-present threat of the ferocious California wildfires.

The cabin sits above the Mill Creek watercourse on steep terrain. The 850-square-foot design was determined by zoning codes, and materials were dictated by additional California-disaster restrictions. The primary living spaces in the small, compact design are on the upper level and were blended together. Fully pocketed, oversized slider-door pairs on opposite sides of the living area allow the area to be doubled with little effort. The "doubling" served to convert an exterior terrace with a sandblasted and serpentine concrete wall into an alfresco dining room. The added pleasures of dining on the terrace are unimpeded views of Mount Saint Helena to the east. Scattered across the fertile fields out below the cabin is a California landscape of another kind: the Dry Creek Valley and its rolling rows of grape-staked vineyards.

The architect accomplished an aesthetic and utilitarian feat with one solution: addressing the high risk of fire—at the same time paying homage to the architecture of Glen Murcutt—he employed the extensive use of metal siding. Because Tom has plans for the uphill portion of the site, the cabin height was kept as minimal as could be with the structure well founded into the hillside. This resulted in the bed, bath, and a small, secluded garden being located on a private level. The foundation was left fully exposed with carefully cast-in-place niches designed for the pleasure and enjoyment of art and votives. Ah, California.

(Lower left) Pocketed living room walls open to increase the living space into the serpentine, sandblasted concrete terrace. (Right) At the opposite side of the great room, large walls open onto a small balcony in the trees.

(Upper left) The bedroom is on the ground level. Slider doors open into a small, landscaped garden. (Lower left) Niches of differing shapes are carved into the concrete wall of the long hallway, which is at ground level. (Opposite) All of the cabinets, shelves, and vanities are of book-matched, English sycamore, which maintains its delicate whiteness.

(Opposite and Right) The great open spaces, inside and out. The vernacular shed structure offers shelter and excitement.

LOGAN CABIN

OWNERS: Eric and Tracey Logan
ARCHITECT: Eric Logan, AIA
PHOTOGRAPHERS: Greg Hursley, Greg Hursley, Inc., Roger Wade

The Logan cabin sits amidst sagebrush in the plains north of Jackson, Wyoming. On two-and-a-half acres in the wide-open spaces of cowboy and ranch country, this 850-square-foot recreational structure is equipped to function as a guesthouse, personal retreat, entertainment hut, and, occasionally, office. But, at any time, it is a place for quiet contemplation.

Ranch-country shed forms abound in this part of the West, many of which lean at a "Keith Richards" angle because of the heavy snow loads. It will take more than a snowstorm and ten feet

of snow to have any effect on the structure of this cozy refuge. Eric designed and built a sturdy structure for informal and bonhomous times with the living, dining, kitchen, and entertainment areas as the focus; that is, if you can take your eyes off the snow-covered peaks and the hand-split rail fences outside. "Servant" and "Served" spaces are separate and distinct. The open living space is clad in cedar paneling, with oxidized steel attachments at the entry, the wood stove, chimney, and the library. The chimney ascends on the exterior and acts as a marker for the site.

The structural solution is a simple and direct post-and-beam system. Steel columns outside the line of enclosure support composite wood and steel beams, which in turn support an expansive sheltering roof. Placing the structure apart from the enclosure allows for a veil of glass to separate the living area from the extreme landscape. A cedar deck projects itself forty feet into the sagebrush.

The interior of the shed is characterized by the exposed structure of the roof plane hovering over the transparent west wall. This is a use of galvanized-steel decking where it

seems to add to the lightness of the roof. Gorgeous, black concrete floors and countertops are a strong contrast to the rawness of the cabinetry, made of medium-density fiberboard. Against the refined yet raw setting, the furnishings become showroom sumptuous; the informal Dakota Jackson dining table and chairs stake their claim and have never before looked more perfectly placed. Tracey, Eric, and their daughters, Isabel and Olivia, have it all going on out here.

(Upper left) The strength of design of the Dakota Jackson table and chairs mingles with a split-rail fence and mountains.
(Right) Interior and exterior become a balance of opposites; the Grand Tetons anchor the design.

(Upper left) Steel columns, rusted steel panels, and glass reflect or disappear into the landscape. (Lower left) Simple cabinet counter space divides the sleeping area from the living room and kitchen areas. (Opposite) Dusk on two and a half acres.

(Opposite and Right) Immense boulders form the footings and foundations. Large peeled tree trunks are used for posts at entries, corners, under overhangs outside, and for interiors.

ADIRONDACK CABIN

OWNERS: Anonymous
ARCHITECTS: Bohlin Cywinsky Jackson:
Peter Bohlin, Royce Earnest, Robert McLaughlin
PHOTOGRAPHER: Karl Backus

This vacation residence, separate garage, and boathouse are arranged along a steeply sloped and forested site at the edge of a mountain lake in upstate New York. The design is in the spirit of the Adirondack Great Camps. Although this style is assumed to be indigenous to the Northeast it was originally derived from influences taken from the alpine traditions of Japan and Europe. The architecture delves into the emotive potential of the materials, especially the large logs and boulders, invoking the mysterious feats of man-made structures such as Stonehenge and the Pyramids. The stone base of this structure rises out of the hillside next to the tree columns, which reach to the sky, embracing the lead-coated copper roof that is a soft reflection of the site.

The approach to the first building offers a glimpse of roof planes and stone verticals through thick pine and hemlock surroundings. The slightly angled main entrance on the upper level bends toward visitors in greeting and welcomes them into a high-rising portico of large peeled logs. The entry passes through a forest of cedar columns toward an exaggerated granite-boulder fireplace. The boulders rise through the rooms as natural sculptural elements to reflect and warm the central living spaces surrounding them.

Light is given by high clerestory windows and streams down through the timber framing and cedar columns as if in the woods. Tree columns, red-pine bark siding, and rustic stick work engage the living spaces with one another as campgrounds would do in a clearing in the forest.

(Upper left) Freehand drawing of the plan. (Upper right) A rustic interior is outfitted with twig furniture; the dining area looks onto a mountain lake. (Lower right) Exaggerated granite boulders of the fireplace rise to mingle with structural ceiling elements above. (Lower left) Site plan. (Opposite) Oversized posts, beams, and boulders are a counterpoint to delicate interior cabinetry, furnishings, and window framing.

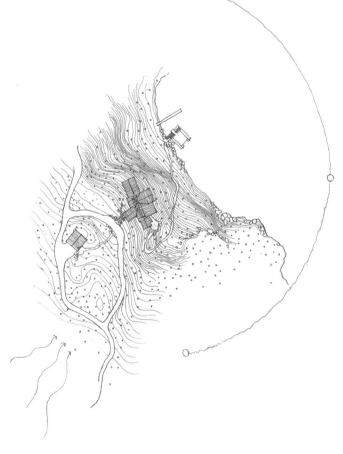

(Upper left) The natural forms and surfaces of timber are shown to coexist with
man-made forms both inside and outside. *(Lower left)* A dragonfly light fixture.
(Opposite) The rustic log boathouse on
the lake shore, with an intricate twig
handrail that leads to the upper level.

(Opposite and Right) The tracery of the tailored geometry emphasizes the delicacy of the natural environment in which it is placed.

RIDDELL CABIN

OWNERS: Lee and Ed Riddell
ARCHITECT: Will Bruder, Will Bruder Architects, Ltd.
Design Team: Richard Jensen, Michael Crooks
PHOTOGRAPHER: Bill Timmerman

Celebrating the needs of a painter, a photographer, their dog Willow, and their shared passion for the outdoors, this modest wooden sculpture is a refined, simply organized pavilion for life, work, and leisure on forested land in Wyoming.

This crisp and tailored plan was conceived and developed from the outside in and the inside out. The taut surfaces of 1" x 3" resawn cedar boards, with their subtle shadow joints, are left to weather—like the simple quiet of a Wyoming shed or the severe rigor of an Anges Martin painting. Set into the cedar siding, flush, polished stainless-steel-framed square windows emphasize the tautness of the exterior surface and hint at the refinement of the interior finish. The reflections of the forest on the glass balance and counter the play of shadows on the texture of the aging cedar skin.

The interiors are finished with smooth, off-white walls, complemented with black slate and maple-strip flooring. Details such as custom-finished maple cabinets, translucent fiberglass shoji screens, and a hot-rolled, black steel-plate fireplace are a part of the architecture. Space is divided between the private and the common. A compressed entry is a gallery of maple, which extends on a diagonal geometry through the house to the living, dining, and kitchen areas. In the entry gallery area the vertical scale opens and large windows frame the striking verticals of an aspen grove beyond the glass. Off the long corridor gallery, blind maple doors conceal private sleeping suites for the owners and for guests. Innovation and detail in spatial arrangements begins at the ridge cap of the cedar-shingle roof and is considered everywhere. The owners' landscape architect, Mother Nature, cherishes the cabin that disappears into her and reflects her best.

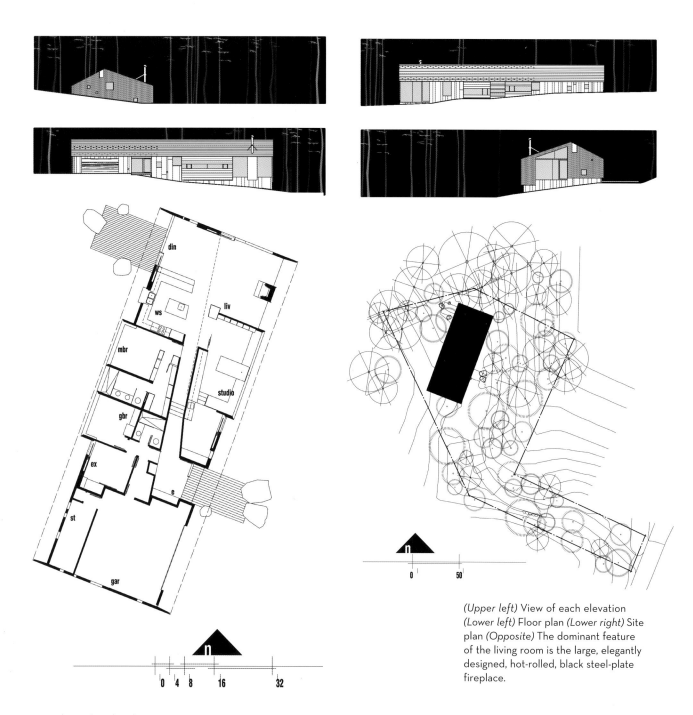

(Upper left) View of each elevation
(Lower left) Floor plan (Lower right) Site
plan (Opposite) The dominant feature
of the living room is the large, elegantly
designed, hot-rolled, black steel-plate
fireplace.

(Upper left) The "compressed" gallery of maple paneling is a diagonal path from the main entrance through the house to the kitchen, dining, and living room areas. (Lower right) A private studio is concealed behind custom-made translucent fiberglass shoji screens. (Lower left) Precision is the main feature of the maple and stainless steel kitchen and work island. (Opposite) The entrance is a balanced composition of volumes and planes.

Long Cabin

OWNERS: Dixon and Ruthanne Long
ARCHITECT: Jim Cutler, AIA, Cutler Anderson Architects
PHOTOGRAPHER: Art Grice

(Opposite) Cedar-log tripods are aesthetically pleasing but, more importantly, serve to withstand the lateral loads behind an envelope of glass. *(Above)* The shed roof almost meets the ground at the rear of the cabin.

In an old-growth forest on the north shore of a saltwater channel is a wonderland getaway for this California couple. The interior and exterior design is made to emphasize natural materials, views of the channel, and the tree-lined shore on the opposite side of the passage. The log tripods and beams on the interior are western red cedar, and the exposed framing is Douglas fir. The simple shed-roof system is of exposed Douglas fir rafters with rigid insulation and a metal roof. The cedar-log tripods are designed to withstand lateral loads; the log beams and 2" x 12" rafters resist gravity. The entire wooden support system is encased in a glass and cedar-shingle shell. The shell is a protective barrier but at the same time reveals the internal workings. To further exhibit the structure and its relationship to the surrounding forest, the cedar tripods are used in front of the uphill windows to introduce the overall concept as one approaches the main entry.

The interiors are open and light-filled, with whitewashed tongue-and-groove southern yellow pine. Ceilings are 1" x 6" tongue-and-groove Douglas fir; the flooring is a lovely European beech. Furnishings tend toward a subtle mid-century modern style, mixed with custom-made wood pieces. Interior half-height tripods near the back of the cabin, where the roofline descends, are bolted into the concrete foundation that surrounds the structure. In the front of the cabin, the foundation becomes a long and broad deck, perfect for dining and relaxing. The simplicity and elegance of this superb hillside cabin is a constant voice in the wilderness.

(*Left*) Kitchen, breakfast nook, and dining areas occupy a coveted, sunny corner. Cabinets are Douglas fir; flooring is European Beech. (*Upper right*) Breathtakingly beautiful cedar tripods create an asymmetrical, lyrical balance in the interior. (*Lower right*) Site plan

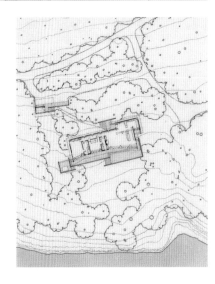

(Upper left) A shed design offers an expansive open face and clerestory. *(Upper right)* Striking detail of the cedar tripod and beam in a glass corner. *(Lower right)* Shed roof of metal and blue cedar shingle siding are exterior finishes. *(Opposite)* The deck and open walls create cabin living at its best.

(Opposite and Right) A year-round getaway tucked into the landscape on the lake.

POINT HOUSE

OWNERS: Anonymous
ARCHITECTS: Bohlin Cywinsky Jackson:
Peter Bohlin, Steve Mongillo, Nguyen Ha
PHOTOGRAPHER: Nic LeHoux

In beautiful western Montana, this cabin beside a lake has all the amenities a family needs for a year-round getaway. Along with the small house is a boat dock, a multipurpose workshop, and a small extra living space. The house is the hub of daily activities, both indoor and those outdoors that the surrounding wild provides, such as tracking, boating, and swimming. The interior is strong and silent, with spaces that provide the necessary serenity and clarity that is desired in a quiet retreat.

Wedged between cedars and pines on a secluded headland, the house nudges up against a granite ledge and reaches west. A wetlands at the end of the stretch is dense with cattail and water flora and is a stopping-off refuge for an increasing number of migrating birds. Orchestral birdsongs and their variations flood the mornings.

The cabin is designed to fit instinctively into an area of pristine forests, natural wetlands, and wildlife habitat, with lake frontage that will remain untrammeled. Seasonal weather extremes in the area call for a very rugged and tolerant design, but one with the sensibilities of poetic environmentalism and humaneness. A long, linear wall with a rusted Cor-Ten steel skin acts to camouflage the site and is an organizing feature of the various design components. Utility functions are on the north; living spaces and a broad wood deck lie to the south. The wall separating the two areas is intentionally blurred with glass, its reflections, and operable panels. Rigorous in detail and delicate in spirit, the Point House is a pavilion among the trees, perfect for gatherings or contemplative solitude.

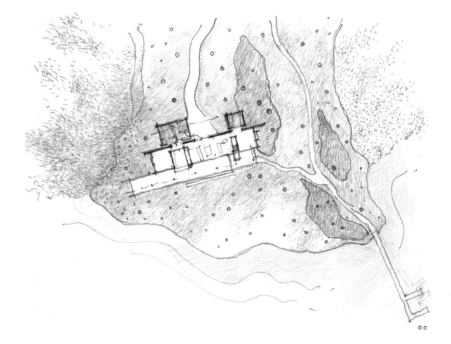

(Lower left) Site plan. *(Upper left)* An elevated platform bed floats in a beautifully articulated "natural" glass corner. *(Upper right)* The living and dining areas share the central open space. The deck runs the length of the lake side of the cabin. *(Opposite)* The living room collects itself around the fireplace. A built-in daybed is perfect for afternoon reading.

(Left) Built-in cabinetry and paneling warm the interior spaces. The slit window breaks the plane of the wall for a natural light source. (Below) The main entry, with a rusted Cor-Ten steel wall that is punctuated by a long slit window. (Right) The bedroom corner projecting into the foliage. A broad overhang protects the structure from snow, sun, or rain. The deck outside is a convenient step away.

PART V   Adaptation

(*Opposite*) An iconic log cabin in an ideal setting has it all. (*Right*) A small loft was made spacious by paring down to the essentials.

ATKINSON / RAMAGE CABIN

OWNERS: William Atkinson and Russ Ramage
ARCHITECT: Depression-era vernacular
PHOTOGRAPHER: François Robert

For the sake of us all, finding the "perfect place" usually translates into making the best of what you've got. Both Russ and William are design professionals who had an idea of building a small, sleek, weekend house. Instead, they found an old cabin on a large, lush lot that needed every loving thing they were well prepared to do. This inspirational getaway an hour from Chicago is an example of ditching certain preconceived notions and turning your reality into a haven.

The tiny, dark interior was stripped down to its cleanest lines where the possibilities began to emerge. Walls and paneling were polished and floors were redone to open the cabin to its maximum interior space, which includes a sleeping loft above. A little brown shed in the back became a part of the extended living area by converting it into a detached meditation-gallery space. Both buildings have lovely vertical, open, wood-framed and -paned windows that add a graceful country touch. The two buildings are connected by a flourish of stone terraces and walkways, which are the foundation for the surrounding gardens and the basic element of future landscaping.

The magic of this refuge is the way the old and the new are perfectly balanced between Iconic and Modern. The furnishings selected for the living room convey the sensation of being in a modern European chateau of indeterminate spaciousness. A large, overhead light fixture mysteriously makes the room seem bigger. The optical illusions of spatial largess are the work of a master, or two. The design secrets employed in William and Russ's cabin are a gift. This is their heaven and it will be forever. It is a work in progress, and we can't wait to see where these talents take us.

(Left) Refinished stairs and windows set the tone to complete an exciting and refined contemporary interior. *(Opposite)* The large overhead light creates a balance of elements, giving a spacious feeling to the room.

(Opposite) The living room gives way to an upper level loft and main level kitchen. The cool perfection is endlessly enjoyable. *(Upper right)* Chandelier and log walls make a romantic backdrop for entertaining close friends. *(Lower right)* Comfort, grace, and insight are found in every vignette.

(*Opposite*) An exotic getaway from the getaway, the tiny teahouse and gallery studio is a travelogue of adventure.
(*Left*) The composition is alluring and reflective, private and generous.

(*Opposite*) Restoration of the "shed" is a journey of perfection and fulfillment. (*Right*) The fascinations of a studio are a meditation in themselves.